Turkeys,
Pilgrims,
and Indian Corn

Other Clarion Books by Edna Barth

Jack-O'-Lantern

Hearts, Cupids, and Red Roses
THE STORY OF THE VALENTINE SYMBOLS

Witches, Pumpkins, and Grinning Ghosts
THE STORY OF THE HALLOWEEN SYMBOLS

Holly, Reindeer, and Colored Lights
THE STORY OF THE CHRISTMAS SYMBOLS

Lilies, Rabbits, and Painted Eggs
THE STORY OF THE EASTER SYMBOLS

I'm Nobody! Who Are You?
THE STORY OF EMILY DICKINSON

TURKEYS, PILGRIMS, and INDIAN CORN

The Story of the Thanksgiving Symbols

by EDNA BARTH

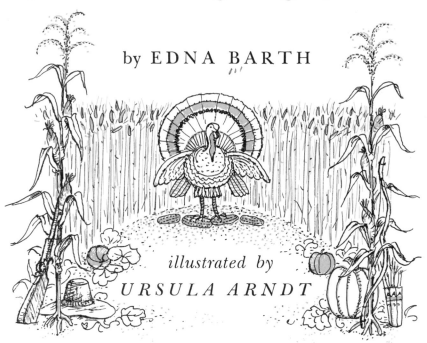

illustrated by URSULA ARNDT

¹⁄₃₉₄.₂₆₈ ₃

A Clarion Book THE SEABURY PRESS • NEW YORK

Library of Congress Cataloging in Publication Data

Barth, Edna.
    Turkeys, Pilgrims, and Indian corn.

    "A Clarion book."
    Bibliography.
    Includes index.
    SUMMARY: Traces the history of this American harvest
celebration and the development of its symbols and legends.
    1. Thanksgiving Day—Juvenile literature.
[1. Thanksgiving Day] I. Arndt, Ursula, ill. II. Title.
GT4975.B37   394.2'683   75-4703
ISBN 0-8164-3149-3

Contents

A stately turkey, groups of Pilgrims and American Indians, the *Mayflower* under full sail. Pumpkins, cornstalks, ears of multi-colored Indian corn, an animal horn overflowing with the fruits of the harvest. All these are symbols of Thanksgiving.

Few of our holidays are as truly American. For Thanksgiving reminds us of the little band of people who founded the Plymouth Colony in Massachusetts. Each November it reopens a favorite chapter in our nation's history.

Compared with the history of most countries, ours is short—less than four hundred years, if we start with the first colonies. It might seem from this that the story of Thanksgiving would be meager. Instead, it is rich and filled with color, for this holiday has its roots in harvest festivals of ancient times and other places.

Three Centuries of Thanksgiving

The Pilgrims' famous feast in 1621 is usually called *The First Thanksgiving*. Dozens of poems, songs, stories, and pageants have been named after it.

Experts now believe that this was not really a day of thanksgiving, but a harvest festival. A true thanksgiving was a day of prayer and fasting.

In either case, it was not the first celebration of its kind on American soil. Forty-three years before, English settlers in Newfoundland had held a harvest festival. Fourteen years before, the Popham Colony in what is now Maine had held one. And three years before the Pilgrim festival, a settlement in Virginia called Berkeley's Hundred named December 4th as a day of thanksgiving to celebrate the safe arrival of some newcomers.

In the autumn of 1621, the people of Plymouth had good reason to celebrate. Less than a year before, worn out from the long voyage in the *Mayflower,* they had landed on these bleak shores, far from their native England. During the first winter, half of the group had died. For a time, it looked as if no one at all would survive.

Now the Pilgrims had eleven houses and

8

four buildings that they shared. They had made friends with a number of Indians. One Indian had taught them how to grow corn. Stored away against the winter, the bumper corn crop was like a promise that the colony would survive.

What better reason for rejoicing? English harvest festivals were one of the Pilgrims' happiest memories. Ancient harvest festivals were mentioned over and over in their Bible:

> *Put ye in the sickle, for the harvest is*
> *ripe;*
> *Come get you down; for the press is*
> *full, the vats overflow.*
> *Joel 3:13*

The only eyewitness to write about the feast of that first autumn was Pilgrim Edward Winslow. "Our harvest being gotten in," he wrote, "our governor sent four men on fowling, that we might after a special manner rejoice together after we had gathered the fruit of our labors."

The four men who were sent "fowling" returned with enough wild turkey, geese, and duck to last almost a week.

The guests, Chief Massasoit and ninety other Indians, stayed for three days of feasting and merrymaking. Several of them went into the woods and shot five deer for the feast.

The Pilgrim men showed off their skill with guns by shooting at a target. The Indian men displayed their skill with the bow and arrow. There were races, wrestling matches, singing, dancing, and games.

Exactly when this great feast took place is uncertain. It was probably about mid-October in the modern, or Gregorian, calendar. The Pilgrims used the old Julian calendar, which ran about ten days earlier.

A year later at "the welcome time of harvest in which all had their bellies filled," there was less cause to rejoice in Plymouth. This time far less than a year's supply of food had been stored away. The Pilgrims were still unused to growing corn, their main crop. Also, they had been too weak to give it the proper care. During the year, they had shared their food with several shiploads of newcomers, and no one had had enough to eat.

The third spring and summer were hot and dry. By July of 1623, the Pilgrims' crops were drying up in the fields. Governor Bradford ordered a day of fasting and prayer. Soon afterward there came a long rain. To celebrate, the governor proclaimed November 29 of that year a day of thanksgiving.

Some say that this, rather than the autumn festival of 1621, was the true beginning of our present Thanksgiving Day.

10

During the years that followed, no one day was set aside in the American colonies for resting and giving thanks. A day would be named when there was some special reason to be thankful. This might be a bumper crop of some kind or escape from an epidemic. The day of thanksgiving might be for a single town or a whole colony. There might be several in one year.

In California, the first thanksgiving is said to have been celebrated in 1769 in the month of July. Mexico, at this time, wanted to keep the British and Russians from gaining control of the Pacific coast. So Mexicans were being sent to found colonies in California.

Of some three hundred Mexicans who set out for San Diego in 1769, only a hundred and twenty-six ever reached it. By this time their food supply was very low and there was danger from hostile Indians. Had it not been for Father Junípero Serra, who came to the Mexicans' rescue, they might all have starved. So, on July 1, Father Serra held a mass of thanksgiving for the survivors.

During the American Revolution, the Continental Congress set aside several days of thanksgiving for victories won. People celebrated in their homes and churches.

When the Constitution was adopted in 1789, President George Washington named

November 26 as a day of thanksgiving. This holiday celebrated the founding of a government that ensured liberty and justice for all. Six years passed before Washington proclaimed another.

Three years after the end of the War of 1812, President Madison proclaimed a day of thanksgiving for peace. From then on until the time of the Civil War, an autumn day of thanksgiving and feasting was observed here and there, mostly in the North.

The holiday was always especially important in New England. There, holidays like Christmas and May Day were considered rowdy. Thanksgiving was the chief holiday.

In time, people came to feel that Thanksgiving Day should be celebrated by the whole nation at the same time. For more than twenty years, Mrs. Sarah Hale, editor of the magazine *Godey's Lady's Book,* urged this in the articles she wrote. She wrote to presidents and to state governors. She made speeches.

The war between the North and South was looming up now. In Sarah Hale's view, a national Thanksgiving Day might help to hold the country together.

At the end of the Civil War, President Abraham Lincoln proclaimed the last Thursday in November as Thanksgiving Day for the whole nation. The presidents who followed issued Thanksgiving Day proclamations, too.

From that time on, Americans have celebrated Thanksgiving much as we do today. Members of families, sometimes joined by family friends, gather for big dinners. Frequently there is a football game or some other sports event in the morning or afternoon. At Thanksgiving services, people of different faiths often worship together.

In some places there are big Thanksgiving Day parades. In New York City, Macy's department store has one for children. Characters from story books, movies, television, and toyland march through the streets. In Phil-

adelphia, Gimbels department store has a similar one. The T. Eaton Company of Canada puts on a mile-long parade in Montreal. In Hollywood, movie and television stars parade in floats.

In schools and churches, the "first Thanksgiving" is acted out in pageants. The one at Plymouth, Massachusetts, takes place outdoors. In pilgrim costume, the players march from Plymouth Rock to the burial hill, where a memorial service is held.

For a time, Canada and the United States celebrated Thanksgiving on the same Thursday in November. Then Canada changed hers to a Monday to make a long weekend. In 1931, it was decided that November was too far beyond harvest time. From then on, the second Monday in October has been Thanksgiving Day in Canada.

Each year in Washington, D.C., there is a Pan-American Thanksgiving celebration. This began in 1919, the first time that the whole western hemisphere had joined together for anything of this kind.

Thanksgiving now falls on the fourth Thursday of November. It is proclaimed each year by the President and the governors of the fifty states. It is a legal holiday throughout the nation, the Canal Zone, Guam, Puerto Rico, and the Virgin Islands.

14

The Pilgrims

Every autumn, as Halloween witches and jack-o'-lanterns disappear from store windows, pilgrims take their places. We see them on Thanksgiving posters, greeting cards, paper tablecloths and napkins, and sometimes in the form of candles or figurines. In American schools, they appear on bulletin boards and classroom windows.

Much has been written about the Pilgrims, but mostly in the past one hundred and fifty years. As late as 1820, outside of the town of Plymouth they were almost unknown.

Governor William Bradford had taken the trouble to write an account of the Pilgrims' experiences. For many years, though, his book, *Of Plimoth Plantation*, was lost, only turning up again in the 1880s.

In the meantime, stories about the Pilgrims had been handed down and were becoming myths. Who were these people who are now so famous that even the youngest school child has heard about them? To know the Pilgrims we must go back to what William

15

Bradford called the "very roote & rise of the same."

The Church of England, at the time of the Pilgrims, stood somewhere between the Catholic and Protestant religions. The services were filled with ritual. The bishops of the church told the members what to believe.

Some members of the church disliked so much ceremony. Also, they wanted to study the Bible and decide for themselves what to believe.

By the early 1600s, thousands of men and women in England, Scotland, and Ireland had come to feel this way. Others made fun of them for wanting to "purify the church." Soon their nickname became the "Puritans."

Most of the Puritans still went to the Church of England. Secretly, they met in homes to study the Bible and listen to sermons. Many of them were content to wait until their side was strong enough to rid the English church of all traces of the Roman Catholic Church.

Other Puritans, known as the Separatists, were prepared to leave the Church of England right away. They wanted a church without deans or bishops or any sacraments except baptism and holy communion. There would be no altars, candles, incense, or organ music.

16

Each church group or congregation would be free to elect its own ministers and elders. Each would manage its own affairs.

In this respect, the Separatists who founded Plymouth differed from the Puritans who later settled around Massachusetts Bay. The Massachusetts Bay Puritans were Presbyterians. In their religion, a *presbytery,* or group of ministers and elders, ruled over the churches of a district.

In the 1600s, the English church and government were one and the same. To separate from the church, therefore, was an act of treason. People were put in jail for it. Several Separatists had even been put to death.

Yet those with enough courage broke away. One such group had been meeting at William Brewster's home in the village of Scrooby, England. When they separated from the Church, life became harder and harder for them. So in 1607 they decided to move to Holland, where they could worship as they pleased.

Leaving England was a problem. No passports were given to "traitors." The voyage would cost money, too, and no one but William Brewster had much.

In spite of obstacles, within a year or so about a hundred and twenty-five Separatists from Scrooby had reached Holland. After a

time in Amsterdam, they moved to Leyden, a center for the spinning and weaving of woolen cloth.

A poor but respected group of more than two hundred by now, they managed to make a living and support their church. Then after ten years or so of this life, they became restless. In England most of them had been farmers. In tiny Holland, farmland was scarce and expensive. Except for a few who had special skills, they were working twelve to fifteen hours a day at low pay.

What was more, their children were forgetting the English language and English ways. They were even losing respect for the Sabbath.

At this time, too, a war was brewing between the Dutch and Spanish.

The Separatists had been longing for a peaceful spot they could call their own. They wanted the chance to earn a decent living and to lead the kind of life described in the New Testament. The time had come, they felt, to make the move.

In February 1620, they finally received a grant for a plantation, as a place to found a colony was called. This was to be near the mouth of the Hudson River in the northern part of what was then the Virginia Colony.

The land would be free, but they needed

18

money for expenses. Hearing about the group, an Englishman named Thomas Weston got together a company of Adventurers, people who backed ventures of this kind.

The Adventurers would put up the money to hire a ship, pay the crew, and buy supplies. In return, the colonists would have to work for the Adventurers for seven years. They could fish, trade in furs with the Indians, cut timber, or do anything that would bring a profit. They would retain only enough to keep them going from year to year. All the rest would go to the Adventurers back in London.

At the end of the seven years, every colonist who was then sixteen or older would be given one share in the company. A share would be worth ten pounds, or about fifty dollars in gold. Each Adventurer would receive one share for every ten pounds he had put into the venture. Thus a person who had toiled for seven years in the Plymouth colony would get no more than a person in London who had invested fifty dollars.

To the future colonists this seemed unfair. They wanted to work for themselves for two days of every week. They also wanted to own their houses and gardens. The Adventurers refused their requests.

Most of the Separatists at Leyden changed

their minds about going to the New World. Fifty dollars worth of real estate in return for seven years of hard labor seemed a poor bargain. Besides, they had just heard about the fate of a hundred and eighty passengers who had set out for Virginia two years before with an English Separatist named Francis Blackwell. Only fifty had survived the voyage.

However, fifty or sixty decided to make the pilgrimage to the New World. For these Pilgrims, as they came to be known, parting with friends and neighbors was very painful. They were even forced to say good-bye to their beloved minister. The Reverend John Robinson had no choice but to stay behind with the bulk of his congregation.

Those who left made their way first to London. After much delay and many problems, they gathered supplies—food, clothing, muskets, powder and shot, axes, and fishing gear.

It was September before they sailed in two ships, the *Mayflower* and the smaller *Speedwell*. However, the *Speedwell* proved unseaworthy, and some of the passengers had to be left behind. The others crowded aboard the *Mayflower*.

Not all of them were going to the New World for religious reasons. The original group had been too small, so other passengers had been rounded up. The Pilgrims called them the Strangers. They called themselves the Saints, a biblical name for one of God's chosen people.

One hundred and two men, women, and children were setting sail for a strange country. Their chances for success seemed slim. It was too late in the year for a fair voyage and too late for planting crops. Their supplies were only scanty. Mostly farmers or craftsmen, the men knew nothing of fishing or fur trading.

But, as one of their spokesmen said, "It is not with us as with other men, whom small things can discourage . . ."

In the figures of Pilgrim men, women, and children that surround us at Thanksgiving time, we have a symbol of this brave and determined spirit.

The Mayflower

Shown a picture or a model of the *Mayflower* under full sail and asked what holiday this suggests, almost any American would say, instantly, "Thanksgiving, of course."

Of all American sailing ships, the *Mayflower* is probably the most famous. Strangely enough, no one knows for sure what she really looked like. Yet we all have a mental image of the ship.

The *Mayflower* had been in the wine trade in France and could carry a cargo of one hundred and eighty tons. At the time of the Pilgrims' voyage, she was probably twenty years old.

A seaworthy ship, the *Mayflower* was fast as well. Her thirty-one-day voyage back to England proves this. A sailing ship of the same size would have trouble in beating this record today.

If the Pilgrims could have left in May as they had planned, they would have had fair winds. As it was, they ran into westerly gales.

22

For days at a time the ship had to lower sails and drift through gigantic seas. Seams in the deck opened, letting icy water down on the frightened passengers, many of whom were ill.

At the height of one gale there was a sound like the boom of a cannon. A main beam in the middle of the ship had buckled and cracked. Several officers wanted to turn back, but the beam was repaired, and the ship's master, Christopher Jones, said that the ship was strong and tight.

The usual route across the Atlantic was the same one Columbus had taken. By this route the *Mayflower* would have sailed to the West Indies, on to Florida, then north along the American coast. Though it was faster, this route meant risking capture by Spanish privateers or being wrecked off Cape Hatteras.

There were ships that had done well sailing straight across the Atlantic, though, so Master Jones had decided to try this route instead.

The exact size of the *Mayflower* is unknown, but a ship of that time that carried a hundred and eighty tons of cargo was around ninety feet long from bow to stern. A ship like this was about twenty-five feet across at the widest point. The middle part of the main deck was open to the weather. Below this was

the gun deck. Below the gun deck was the hold.

At bow and stern were high structures. The one at the bow was called the forecastle. Here the crew slept, and the cook had a brick, wood-burning stove.

The high structure aft, the sterncastle, had two short decks, one below the other. In one of these was the master's stateroom and the "great cabin," where the officers ate. In both, there were also bunks for the more important passengers. Since this was the driest part of the ship, the flour and seabiscuits were stored here, too.

24

On the deck below was the steerage. Steering wheels and gear had not yet been invented. Instead, the ship was steered by a whipstaff, a beam attached to the tiller that ran through a sternpost down to the rudder.

Some of the passengers slept in the shallop, an open boat that was stowed on the gun deck. Perhaps there were hammocks and double or triple bunks for some of the others. Most of the passengers probably spread blankets on the planking that formed the floors of the decks. In any case, no one had much privacy. Every inch of the ship was crammed.

Beside food, clothing, and some pieces of furniture, the Pilgrims took along a supply of seeds, garden tools, saws, axes, hammers, gunpowder, and firearms. For trading with the Indians, they had barrels of bright cloth, beads, knives, and small mirrors.

Christopher Jones was an expert mariner. For twelve years he had commanded the *Mayflower*. By the time of this voyage, he had bought a quarter share in the ship. The Pilgrims seem to have liked and respected him.

Beside the ship's master and several officers, there were twenty or more seamen. Mostly a rough lot, they cursed at the Pilgrims and made fun of them for their constant praying. One sailor threatened to throw sick pas-

25

sengers to the sharks, then take their belongings. As it turned out, he got sick himself and died at sea.

The Pilgrims saw the hardships aboard ship as God's way of testing their faith and courage.

After more than two months at sea, land was finally sighted. Joy swept through the ship. They were at Cape Cod, north of their goal, the mouth of the Hudson River. Heading south, they ran into shoals and roaring breakers. Trying to reach the Hudson seemed too dangerous. So they took shelter instead in what is now Provincetown Harbor, at the end of Cape Cod.

26

The ship at anchor, the Pilgrims fell to their knees and gave thanks for their safe arrival. Here in Provincetown Harbor, the Pilgrim leaders drew up the *Mayflower Compact*. Some of the "Strangers" had been talking about going off on their own once they landed. Somehow, the Pilgrims convinced them that, unless everyone stuck together, all might perish. Most of the able-bodied men who were of age signed the Compact. They agreed to stay together and obey whatever laws were made.

After exploring Cape Cod, the Pilgrims decided that this was not the best place for them to settle. There were too many Indians around and not enough fresh water.

Instead, they decided to explore a place to the north, which they had heard about from a *Mayflower* crew member. Known as Thievish Harbor, the spot was so named because an Indian there had once stolen a harpoon from an English mariner. Thievish Harbor was probably what is now Gloucester, Massachusetts, but the Pilgrims never found it. They landed instead at a place they named Plymouth, after the English seaport from which they had set sail.

If the *Mayflower* had returned to England that winter, the colony might well have failed, for without the shelter the ship offered, more of the Pilgrims might have died. When they moved ashore, the sight of the ship in the harbor made them feel safer. They knew that, if danger came, they could go aboard and sail away.

When the *Mayflower* finally returned to England the following April, the Pilgrims were on their own, three thousand miles from home. With spring came the fragrant pink trailing arbutus, which they promptly named mayflower. The large stream that flowed into Plymouth they named Jones River after the ship's master.

Today, lying at a pier in Plymouth, Massachusetts, is a full scale model of the *Mayflower*. Exhibits with life-size figures show what life must have been like on the sixty-six day voyage.

This replica, known as *Mayflower II,* was built in England in 1956. She sailed across the Atlantic under the command of Captain Alan Villiers. The crossing took fifty-three days, only thirteen days less than it took the first *Mayflower*.

The Pilgrim Fathers

Ten years after *Mayflower I* crossed the Atlantic, Governor William Bradford wrote, "Our Fathers were Englishmen which came over this great ocean, and were ready to perish in the wilderness; but they cried unto the Lord, and He heard their voice."

Among the men known as the Pilgrim Fathers was *William Brewster*. It was his family manor house at Scrooby, England, that served as a meeting place for the Separatists of the area. A graduate of Cambridge University, he was probably the only Pilgrim with a college education. In Holland, Brewster supported himself by teaching and by publishing religious books that were forbidden in England. With William Bradford he returned to England and got the Pilgrims a patent from the Virginia Company for the land in America.

While the Pilgrims were in Holland, Brewster was the ruling Elder of their church. Since the Reverend Robinson could not sail with them, William Brewster took his place. Until 1629, when a minister was appointed in Plymouth, Elder Brewster preached two sermons every Sunday.

29

William Brewster was fifty-seven, much older than most of the Pilgrims who sailed in the *Mayflower*. As far as we know, they were mostly in their mid-twenties. Brewster lived to be eighty, working in the fields well into old age.

John Carver, the Pilgrims' first governor, was one of the richest *Mayflower* passengers. Like Brewster, he was older than the others, forty-five. Before joining the Pilgrim church, Carver had been a London merchant. He spent almost all his fortune on expenses the Adventurers refused to pay. His wife and six servants went with him to Plymouth.

Carver was the main agent in chartering the *Mayflower* and making arrangements for the voyage.

While the *Mayflower* was in Provincetown Harbor, John Carver was elected governor by the Pilgrim men. The women had no vote. John Carver was respected by all the Pilgrims for his courage and good judgment. His positive outlook seemed to inspire others.

In January and February of the first winter, sometimes two or three people died in a single day. Many died of scurvy, a sickness caused by lack of fresh vegetables and fruits. Some probably died of pneumonia and some of typhus, a disease carried by lice.

30

At times there were only six or seven people who were well enough to care for all the rest. While he was able, Governor Carver did his share of nursing the sick. By this time they were stretched out in the storehouse and aboard the *Mayflower,* which had become a hospital ship.

For a time Governor Carver himself was laid low. He recovered but remained weak. Yet when spring came, he labored in the fields like everyone else. Then one day in April he suffered a stroke and died.

The next November a letter came from Thomas Weston, head of the London Adventurers. He scolded Carver for not having sent back any cargo in the *Mayflower.*

After John Carver's death, *William Bradford* became governor. Except for five years, he held this office until his death in 1657.

31

William Bradford grew up in a village in Yorkshire, England, in a family of well-to-do farming people. There were no schools in the area, but somehow he learned to read and write. By the time he was twelve, he was reading the Bible with great interest. Services in the Church of England lacked meaning for him. So, before long, he was going to secret meetings at nearby Scrooby.

There he listened to William Brewster and others. When they decided to separate from the official church, William Bradford joined them. Still in his teens, he explained to his relatives that he knew how much this hurt them, but he also knew he was doing right.

Mostly self-educated, William Bradford could read and speak Dutch, French, and Latin. At sixty, he began teaching himself Hebrew. He wanted to be able to read the Old Testament in the original tongue.

As governor, Bradford was also judge and constable. This gave him a great deal of power, but he gladly shared the power with those who could share his duties. For many years he took no pay for his work. In fact, he paid many of the official expenses out of his own pocket.

In 1630 the busy governor began what he called his "Scribled Writings." Now known as

Of Plimouth Plantation, it tells of events in the colony between 1620 and 1647.

For over a hundred years the manuscript was handed down in Bradford's family. Then it was given to a Boston minister. The minister kept it in his library in the tower of the Old North Church.

During the American Revolution, the church was used as a stable by the British; when they left, Bradford's manuscript and other papers were missing. Some of his letters turned up a few years later in a grocery store in Nova Scotia. They were being used as wrapping paper for pickles, soap, cheese, and butter!

Not until 1855 did Bradford's long-lost manuscript turn up in the library of a palace near London. It was published in Boston the following year. This was really the beginning of Pilgrim history. For William Bradford's book gave us most of what we know about the Pilgrims and early Plymouth. His "Scribled Writings" became recognized as one of the great books of the seventeenth century.

Edward Winslow, another leading Pilgrim, served as governor several times when William Bradford declined. In 1623 Winslow was sent back to England to round up more people for the colony.

On another visit, thirteen years later, Winslow found England under Cromwell so pleasant that he decided to stay there. At this time England had no king, and Cromwell, the "Lord Protector," believed in freedom of religion. He gave Winslow a high post and sent him on a mission of war to the Caribbean. There Winslow died of tropical fever.

Samuel Fuller was the Pilgrims' doctor. He had brought along surgeon's tools and some "physic"—laxatives and other medicines. He had no cure for scurvy or pneumonia. In the 17th century, no doctor did. Some of the medicines in use then did more harm than good. The Pilgrim women, like other women of the time, brewed their own medicines from herbs. With these, they treated colds and all common aches and pains.

Dr. Fuller went to Plymouth without his wife and child, sending for them later. He died thirteen years after Plymouth was founded.

Perhaps best known among Pilgrim men are *Miles Standish* and *John Alden,* who were not Separatists at all. Miles Standish never did become a full member of the Pilgrims' church. A seasoned soldier, he was hired to go along and train the Pilgrims to defend themselves.

Captain John Smith, a founder of Jamestown in Virginia, had asked for the job. Smith

34

had been to New England, as he called the northern part of the vast Virginia colony. He had described it in a book and made a map of it. The Pilgrims decided not to hire Captain Smith, but to take his book with them instead. It was "better cheap than he," they said.

Miles Standish proved a good choice. A strong man, he himself escaped the "Great Sickness" of the first winter, but he lost his wife, Rose Standish. With others who remained well, he took tender care of the sick and ailing when the *Mayflower* became a hospital ship.

The first spring, uneasy about the Indians, the Pilgrims made Standish their captain. Under his training, the men all became expert shots.

Barely five-feet-two in his boots, Miles Standish had red hair and a fiery temper. Behind his back he was sometimes called Captain

Shrimp. He was afraid of nothing, except making proposals of marriage—if one can believe Henry Wadsworth Longfellow's poem of 1858, *The Courtship of Miles Standish.*

In the poem, the bluff, middle-aged

soldier wishes to marry Priscilla Mullins. Instead of asking her himself, he sends young John Alden to speak for him. To this, Priscilla replies with the famous line, "Why don't you speak for yourself, John?"

Miles Standish learned the Indian language and could act as go-between when the Pilgrims and Indians had something to discuss.

In 1632, after Plymouth was on its feet, he and several others founded the town of Duxbury, about ten miles north of Plymouth. There, on Captain's Hill is a monument to Miles Standish.

Among the supplies the Pilgrims took with them on the *Mayflower* was beer. *John Alden,* a cooper, was hired to make the barrels to hold it and to go along and keep them from leaking.

As everyone knows, John Alden stayed on in Plymouth and married Priscilla Mullins; like Miles Standish, the Aldens later moved to Duxbury. And, like Standish, John Alden did some surveying.

John and Priscilla Alden had eleven children and many grandchildren. John lived to be eighty-seven. Priscilla lived several years after his death. Their descendents number in the thousands.

The only holiday in memory of the people who founded the Plymouth colony is Forefathers' Day. First celebrated in 1769, it is still observed today in the town of Plymouth each December 11th.

The Pilgrim Mothers

At early Plymouth the women had no voice or vote at all. Their husbands did the voting, made the decisions, and signed any important papers. As the "Pilgrim Fathers," they receive all the credit for founding Plymouth.

Eighteen Pilgrim women crossed the stormy Atlantic with their husbands to face a New England winter. The cold, dirty, crowded cabin of the *Mayflower* was hardly the best place for a child to be born. Yet, Elizabeth Hopkins and Susannah White both gave birth to babies.

By spring only six of the eighteen married women who had come to Plymouth were still alive. They were Ellen Billington, Mary Brewster, Katherine Carver, a woman listed as Mrs. Edward Fuller, Elizabeth Hopkins, and Susannah White.

Susannah White's husband, William, had died in February leaving her with a five-year-old son, Resolved, and the baby boy, Peregrine, who was born while the *Mayflower* was in Provincetown Harbor. In May, Susannah mar-

38

ried Edward Winslow, who had lost his own wife.

Now, as Susannah Winslow, she made their one-room house as homelike as she could. In one corner was the wicker cradle she had brought along for her new baby. Against one wall was a cabinet to hold blankets and clothing. Susannah had also brought along a few pretty things—pink satin slippers and a satin cape.

Susannah White not only survived the hardships of the first winter, with a newborn infant to nurse and care for. She lived to be eighty-five, something unusual at that time when so many women died young.

Hard as the *Mayflower* voyage had been on Susannah White, at least she had her children with her. *Dorothy Bradford* had waved good-bye in Holland to five-year-old John, her only child. She had wanted to bring John, but his father insisted on waiting until they had a decent home for the little boy.

Dorothy Bradford prayed for courage, but the separation from her child was too much for her. One day while the *Mayflower* lay in Provincetown Harbor, Dorothy, in a fit of despair, slipped overboard and drowned.

Whether this was an accident or something she did on purpose, no one was ever sure.

Elizabeth Hopkins was married to Stephen Hopkins. She had two stepchildren, and a little girl of her own. Her baby boy, Oceanus, was born as the *Mayflower* was crossing the Atlantic.

When Oceanus died before he was two, his mother was heartbroken. Elizabeth Hopkins was sure that her child would have lived had he had milk to drink and some better food.

The fact that few children died during the first winter is probably because of the good care their mothers gave them. Weak and sick as they were themselves, the mothers doctored their children with medicines brewed from herbs. And, somehow, they must have managed to keep them warm.

The Pilgrim Fathers were brave and determined men. Had they come alone, it is likely that they would have survived. But how much harder it would have been without the stronghearted women who cooked and sewed for them, nursed them in sickness, loved them, and shared their faith.

Pilgrim Children

On some of our Thanksgiving greeting cards, instead of grown-up Pilgrims, we find Pilgrim children. Their faces may be serious, but just as often they are full of fun and mischief.

Of the ninety-nine people who landed at Plymouth, about thirty were children. Some were only babies. Others were nearly grown. Best known, perhaps, are the two boys born aboard the *Mayflower,* Oceanus Hopkins and Peregrine White, whose name means pilgrim. Peregrine lived to be eighty-three. Years after his birth, as the "first English born in these parts," he was given a tract of land. Oceanus, as we have read, lived only until the second spring.

Some of the children, the Hopkins and Chiltons for example, were with their parents.

Others had come with more distant relatives. A number of children came as servants.

Among these were Richard, Jasper, and Ellen More, and a little brother whose name is unknown. These "bound children" were supposed to work for seven years for the family that had brought them.

Ellen More came with the Winslows, and Jasper with the Carver family. Richard was bound to the Brewster family.

Jasper died aboard the *Mayflower* in Provincetown Harbor. Ellen and the little brother died the first winter. Only Richard survived.

Among the teenagers were Elizabeth Tilley, who was fourteen, Giles Hopkins, thirteen, Constance Hopkins and Mary Chilton, who were both fifteen.

Most of the Pilgrim children had common English names like John or Elizabeth. A few were named for the hopes and beliefs of their parents. Among these were boys named Resolved White and Love and Wrestling [with the Devil] Brewster. Remember Allerton and Humility Cooper were two of the girls.

More than three months after they had left Europe, the Pilgrim children finally found themselves at the site of their new home. It was December, a month when modern children look forward to Christmas. But there

42

would be no holiday for the children of Plymouth. Not in 1620 or in the years to follow. Christ's birthday was considered a solemn event, not a time for "rowdy" fun.

After months in the crowded cabins of the *Mayflower,* the children must have been happy to be free to run and jump and shout. They probably explored the brook that flowed into the harbor and the Indian cornfields cleared for planting. Then there was the slope where the houses would be built and the big hill with its fine view of the bay and ocean.

It was said that wild beasts and savage Indians lurked in the woods that crept close to the rugged shore. Some of the children must have been fearful.

While most of the children survived the first winter, many lost one or even both parents. These orphans were taken in by other families. They were considered servants, but Pilgrim servants were part of the family.

For American children today, Thanksgiving and the days that follow are a welcome vacation from school. For the children of Plymouth, the three-day festival in 1621 was a chance to eat all they wanted and enjoy a welcome vacation from work.

There was no such thing as school. The most a good many of them ever learned was some simple arithmetic, how to write their names, and read the Bible a little.

Pilgrim children were needed to do work. From the moment they could walk, they were part of the family team. A small boy could be taught to pull weeds, gather nuts and berries, or pick up kindling. The smallest girl might be put to work rocking the baby's cradle. As soon as she could handle needles, she learned to sew seams and knit stockings.

Older girls did the same kind of work as their mothers—spinning, weaving, pounding corn into meal, making soap and candles, cooking and baking.

By helping the men, a boy learned how to fell trees, how to saw and split wood for building houses, how to sow and reap crops, to fish and to hunt.

Among the Plymouth children were two lively brothers named John and Francis Billington. While the *Mayflower* was still anchored off Provincetown, John pried open a keg of gunpowder and nearly blew up the ship.

During the first winter Francis climbed a tall tree and saw what looked to him like an ocean. All excited, he ran home to announce that he had discovered the Pacific. This turned

44

out to be a large pond, which the Pilgrims named Billington's Sea. It still goes by that name today.

In July, John caused excitement by getting lost in the woods. For five days he lived on wintergreen and partridge berries and anything else he could find. Finally, he was found by Indians of the Nauset tribe. They took care of him until the Pilgrims tracked him down.

At least a hundred Nausets waded out to the Pilgrims' boat. John was carried piggyback by Aspinet, the Nauset chief. Around John's neck were strings of wampum—gifts from the Nausets.

The Pilgrim children created their own amusements. They whittled toys out of wood, made dolls out of rags, cornhusks, or pinecones. They invented games.

Fishing and clamming were useful, but they were also good sport. Picking berries or gathering nuts in a group could be fun, too. In summer, when their parents could spare them, young people enjoyed swimming.

Pilgrim children were up by sunrise—in winter even earlier. Breakfast might be ready, but before they sat down, the head of the household read a chapter from the Bible and asked a blessing.

After breakfast, everyone young and old got to work. Sometime near sunset the father or head of the household returned for the night. Before he ate, he had the children recite their ABC's and asked them questions about religion from the catechism.

The day ended with a prayer and another chapter of the Bible. By this time only the older boys and girls would still be up.

Pilgrim children had strict parents. They were taught to fear God, respect the king and governor, and be proud of being English. They were in this world for a purpose, they were told. If they feared God and did their best to obey the commandments, they could look forward to another life after death.

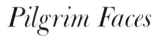

Pilgrim Faces

Pilgrims have been pictured so often in paintings and in books that we may think we know how they looked. Actually, we know almost nothing about their looks. They lived long before the days of the camera. At that time people who could afford it had their portraits painted. The others left no record of what they looked like.

Of those who sailed on the *Mayflower,* only Edward Winslow ever had his portrait painted. It was done in England thirty years after the landing at Plymouth. A pleasant-looking man, he wore his hair parted on the side and had a mustache and goatee.

Miles Standish was described in a book by Thomas Morton of the settlement called Merry Mount, near Boston. From it we learn that Captain Standish was a short man with red hair. There is no description of any other *Mayflower* passengers. At that time beards were in style in England, so the Pilgrim men probably wore them.

The women and older girls probably wore their long hair tucked under linen caps. What their faces were like we can only imagine. For a time, few of the Pilgrims could be very sure of this themselves. They could only look into a brook or a barrel of water or see a vague reflection in one of the metal mirrors that some of them had brought along.

Artists have often pictured all of them as thin-lipped people with grim expressions. The chances are that they differed in feature and expression as much as any other group of people.

Pilgrim Clothes

A favorite symbol of Thanksgiving, the Pilgrims shown in pictures or as figures are usually dressed much alike. The men and boys wear black suits with white collars and cuffs. Their tall black hats have broad brims and a silver buckle for decoration. Their shoes are buckled, too. The women and girls wear white aprons and caps, with long dresses in drab colors.

From this came the idea that bright colors went against the Pilgrims' religion.

Nothing could be further from the truth. Along with the wills that the Pilgrims left were lists of their belongings. These included their clothing. The lists show that the Pilgrims dressed like people of the same class in England. They wore simple but colorful clothes. The only Pilgrim who had many black clothes was Elder Brewster. But he also owned a violet cloak, a pair of green trousers, and a red cap.

Of the other men, those who had been well-to-do owned a black suit and hat for Sunday, and sometimes black shoes. It is doubtful that either hat or shoes had silver buckles on them. Not a single buckle is mentioned in any list.

On weekdays the men wore gray, brown, or blue linen shirts and woolen or leather breeches. Their knit stockings came up to their hips. When it was chilly, the men wore sleeveless leather jackets.

The usual hat was a wool stocking cap known as a Monmouth cap. Instead of coats the Pilgrim men had sleeveless cloaks that left their arms free. Most of these clothes were colored.

The women's and girls' clothes were even brighter. Their dresses might be red, purple, bright blue, or green. Made with full skirts, the dresses reached to their ankles. Under a laced bodice they wore a "stomacher" of a different color or material. In cold weather they wore waistcoats, which were usually red. For outdoors they had cloaks with hoods.

Until a boy was six years old, he wore a dress, which was called a coat. Aside from that,

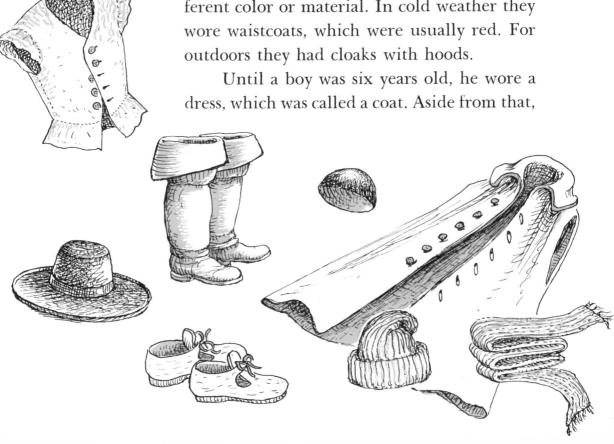

there were no special clothes for children. They were dressed to look like small adults. And, like the adults, they were dressed in colors.

How then did the idea grow up that the Pilgrims wore only gray, black, or dun-colored garments?

At least one list attached to a Pilgrim will mentioned "one sad colored suit and cloak." This may have led to the idea that clothes were drab. But, at that time a "sad color" meant a deep color. Mulberry, a deep red, was "sad," and so were nut-brown or forest green.

For the first few years there was no time in the Plymouth Colony to grow the flax needed to make linen. And there were no sheep yet to furnish wool. The garments the Pilgrims had brought with them were becoming threadbare. So the women mended and patched, and patched and mended. One

stanza of a Pilgrim ballad tells how they *clouted,* or patched, their garments. Sometimes they even patched a patch or, as they said it, put a "clout upon a clout."

> And now our garments begin to grow
> thin,
> And wool is much wanted to card and
> to spin;
> If we can get a garment to cover with-
> out,
> Our other in-garments are clout upon
> clout;
> Our clothes we brought with us are
> often much torn,
> They need to be clouted before they
> are worn;
> But clouting our garments they hin-
> der us nothing,
> Clouts double are warmer than single
> whole clothing!

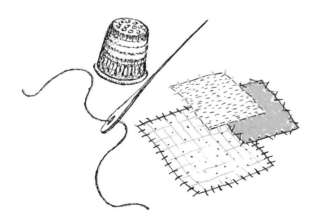

Pilgrim Animals

There was no room aboard the *May-flower* for cattle or other livestock, but at least two dogs sailed with the Pilgrims. One was a mastiff and one a spaniel.

At Provincetown, Miles Standish led an exploring party ashore. As the men were walking along the beach, they saw six Indians and a dog. The Indian dog wanted to make friends with the spaniel, but the Indians were afraid of the strangers with guns. They ran off into the woods, whistling to their dog to follow them.

John Goodman and Peter Browne took both dogs along one day when they went to cut bulrushes for roof-thatching. The dogs suddenly took off after a deer. The young men followed them deep into the woods and lost their way.

By nighttime it had begun to snow. Taking shelter under a tree with the dogs, the young men were terrified by the howling of wolves. They thought these were lions.

When they got back to Plymouth, John's feet were swollen with frostbite and his shoes had to be cut off. Undaunted, he limped off to

53

the woods again with the spaniel a few days later. This time, two wolves tried to attack the dog. John held the wolves off with a stick. He reported that "they sat on their tails grinning at me a good while, then went away."

When the Pilgrims buried fish with the corn they planted, they didn't know that the dogs could smell it. The mastiff and spaniel dug it up and, with it, a good deal of newly planted corn. They had to be tied up until the corn was high.

By 1622 the Pilgrims had sent to England for chickens and geese and were raising their own. Before long they learned how to tame wild turkey and began to raise these as well. Goats gave the Pilgrims milk and meat. By this time they had sheep, too, to furnish wool for clothing.

In 1625, Governor Bradford wrote in a letter to Robert Cushman in England that the people of Plymouth "never felt the sweetness of the country until this year." Now that the Pilgrims had animals, their standard of living was much better. Mothers could get milk for their children.. An old pig or cow could be slaughtered and salted down for use throughout the winter. The animal fat gave the Pilgrims tallow for making candles.

Pilgrim Houses

The log cabin has become a kind of symbol of our pioneering past. Until fairly recently, storybooks usually showed the Pilgrims living in this kind of house. The truth is that the Pilgrims had never seen a log cabin. The first ones in the New World were built by the Swedish settlers on the shores of Delaware Bay, in the 1640s.

The Pilgrims' houses were built of sawed pine boards. The posts that formed the framework and beams were made of oak. The roofs were made of bulrush thatch.

The first building, begun late in 1620,

55

was a storehouse called the Common House. By January it was serving as a hospital. The Common House done, the men began building small, one-room houses. As sickness began to strike, more and more of the men were unable to work. Sometimes only six were well enough.

Meanwhile, besides building the houses, the men helped care for the sick and buried the dead—at night so the Indians would not notice.

In April, when the Mayflower returned to England, there were seven little houses along a rough road that led to the burial hill. The Pilgrims named it Leyden Street, after the city where so many of them had lived in Holland.

Some of the houses had sleeping lofts. Others had just one room, which was none too large. Against one wall was a large fireplace built of wood daubed with clay. Fireplaces like this caught on fire at times, but the Pilgrims had no bricks and no time to build stone fireplaces. The main thing was to have shelter while they planted the crops that would keep them alive.

Orphans and single men moved in with various families. The Pilgrims were nearly as crowded ashore as they had been aboard the

Mayflower. But at least there was solid ground under their feet. What is more, spring had come. The air was mild now and filled with birdsong. Snug in their little houses, the Pilgrims took new hope.

Today, visitors to Plymouth, Massachusetts, can see how the village looked in its early days. The first houses are no longer standing on Leyden Street. But, three miles away on a slope overlooking the water, is *Plimoth Plantation*. Here are copies of the houses that stood in Plymouth in 1627. On the hill behind them is a model of the fort and the cannon that protected the village. The ground floor of the fort served as the Pilgrims' church.

Sheep and chickens wander about freely. In the kitchen gardens are the same kinds of herbs and flowers that grew here so long ago. People in Pilgrim garb help bring the Pilgrim world to life. Men may be seen thatching roofs or cutting wood in a pine grove. Women may be found pounding corn into meal, cooking over open fires, carding wool, or working in the gardens.

As they work, the women and men answer questions and describe the life that once went on here.

Plymouth Rock

Most of us have seen at least one picture of men, women, and children in Pilgrim clothes, stepping ashore onto a granite boulder. A painting or drawing of such a scene makes us think at once of Plymouth and perhaps of the first Thanksgiving.

No landmark on our shores is more famous than Plymouth Rock, but this was not always so. Until shortly before the American Revolution, it was just another granite boulder near the shore. During the next century it was hauled first to Town Square, then to Pilgrim Hall, a museum in Plymouth.

Finally it was brought back to the waterfront. There, with a box supposed to contain Pilgrim bones, it was placed under a stone canopy.

58

In 1920 Plymouth celebrated its 300th anniversary. At that time, to keep souvenir hunters from chipping off bits of granite, the rock was placed in a pit protected with an iron railing. Overhead, sheltering visitors from the weather, is a portico.

Whether the Pilgrims really stepped ashore onto this particular rock is open to question. But perhaps that is unimportant. Plymouth Rock is a symbol—a symbol of faith and hope and of something to be relied on. As such, it might be called a symbol of the Pilgrims themselves, the brave men, women, and children who worked together to found Plymouth.

Indian Neighbors

To most of us, Pilgrims and American Indians shown together are a familiar symbol of Thanksgiving. Such Indians have often been portrayed wearing feathered bonnets, with blankets draped around their shoulders. This is as false as some of the pictures of the Pilgrims.

No Indians east of the Mississippi wore feathered bonnets. The Indian men around Plymouth and others the Pilgrims knew wore their hair in a crest running from front to back. Tucked into the crest at a jaunty angle there was usually an eagle feather.

Unless it was cold, the Indian men wore nothing but deerskin aprons. In the cold weather they wore deerskin moccasins, or moccasins and leggings, and deerskin mantles. At Plymouth, Massachusetts, a statue of Chief Massasoit shows how a Wampanoag Indian man really looked.

Indian women wore deerskins wrapped around their waists like skirts. When it was cold, young girls wore beaver coats. Older women wore coats of deerskin.

The Pilgrims saw their first Indians near Provincetown when Miles Standish and his men went ashore to explore. When the Indians ran away, the Pilgrims followed their tracks until dark. Then they camped in the woods

60

overnight. The next day they went as far as what is now Truro. On their way back they found Indian graves and some Indian corn.

On another trip ashore they discovered more graves and their first Indian houses, all of them empty. These houses were not the wigwams that we sometimes see in pictures. They were long lodges with curved roofs.

At Plymouth a party of men went ashore to explore the coast. They covered seven or eight miles but saw no Indians or any houses. What they did find were cleared fields covered with stubble. They knew from this evidence that Indians had lived there not long before.

There was no sign of a live Indian at Plymouth until the middle of February. Then, a Pilgrim hunting for wildfowl saw a dozen Indian men walking in a single file toward the settlement. Nothing came of this, but the Pilgrims were alarmed. There was no reason to expect the Indians to be friendly. In the past, fishermen and traders from Europe had often treated them very badly.

Following this incident, the Pilgrims made Miles Standish their captain. Master Jones let them have a cannon from the *Mayflower*. This they mounted on the big hill where their dead were buried.

As it turned out, there were still Indians

61

fifteen or twenty miles away from the Pilgrims, but they were too weak to attack the settlement. Like the Indians who had formerly lived at Plymouth, these Indians had suffered from serious sickness. The white traders and fishermen had been bringing their own diseases with them. These might have been nothing more than mumps or measles. But to people exposed to them for the first time, such diseases could be deadly.

Any settlement in the New World needed at least one Indian friend and ally. The Pilgrims were lucky in finding a friend early. This was Samoset, who strode into Plymouth nearly naked one mild day in early March.

"Welcome, Englishmen," he said, holding out his right hand.

Samoset was the first Indian the Pilgrim children had seen, so they probably stared at him with great interest. The grown-ups were pleased to find that Samoset spoke English, and made him welcome. Then they treated him to wild duck and some of their precious sea-biscuit, cheese, and butter.

Samoset was a leader of the Pemaquid Indians on the coast of what is now Maine. He had learned the language from English fishermen. Two days later, Samoset returned with five Wampanoag Indians. Like Samoset, they enjoyed the English food the Pilgrims served. To show their thanks they danced and sang for their hosts and hostesses.

The Indians had brought along some skins to trade, but this was the Pilgrims' sabbath. Business and entertainment were both forbidden. So they gave the Indians some presents and told them to come back on a weekday.

A few days later, Samoset brought an Indian named Squanto to Plymouth. The sole survivor of the Pawtuxet tribe of the Plymouth area, Squanto had spent several years in England and could speak the language.

Squanto told the Pilgrims that Massasoit, chief of the Wampanoags, would like to meet them. A meeting was arranged, and Massasoit received a royal welcome. The Pilgrims, he was told, were ready to make a treaty of peace in the name of King James of England.

Massasoit was led to a partly finished house and was seated on a pile of cushions. Then, to the blare of a trumpet and a ruffle of drums, Governor Carver entered. A feast of roast venison was served. After that the governor and the Indian chief smoked a peace pipe and made a treaty. They agreed to live in peace and to help each other in case of attack.

Governor Carver went with Massasoit as far as the town brook where they embraced and parted. Then Massasoit's brother took his place. The whole ceremony, except for the treaty-making, was repeated, including a second feast.

Massasoit needed the Pilgrims as much as they needed him. Half of his people had died in the Great Sickness. Now he lived in fear of the Narragansett Indians, who had all been spared.

According to Edward Winslow's journal, Massasoit always told the truth. He was never cruel and used reason rather than force to rule his people. Without his loyalty and good will, the settlement at Plymouth might never have survived the next few years.

Alone in the world, Squanto decided to stay with the Pilgrims. It was he who introduced them to the maize or corn that became their mainstay. Squanto taught them which wild herbs and berries were safe to eat, how to fish, and how to trade with the Indians for beaver furs.

As time went on, the Pilgrims found out that Squanto was spreading rumors. The Pilgrims, he said, had buried the Indian sickness in the ground and could dig it up whenever they wanted. He himself, he claimed, could set the Pilgrims against the Indians. The other Indians believed Squanto. They were paying him bribes to keep him friendly.

In spite of this, the Pilgrims kept Squanto with them. Through him, they could keep track of the mood of the other Indians.

Sometime during that first year another Indian came to Plymouth to live. His name was Hobomok.

The Pilgrims made good use of the rivalry that sprang up between Squanto and the newcomer. As the two Indians vied for standing, Governor Bradford pretended to favor one and Miles Standish the other. No matter what Squanto and Hobomok did on the sly, they were useful. They brought the Pilgrims news of Indian doings, and they served as go-betweens.

One day Squanto and Hobomok got into a fight with an Indian named Corbitant and some of his men. Hobomok broke away and ran back to Plymouth. There he reported that Corbitant was going to kill Squanto for being friendly to the white people.

The Pilgrims knew that, if they let this go by, all the Indians would lose respect for them. So several men were sent out. If they found Squanto dead, they were to cut off Corbitant's head.

Luckily, Squanto was still alive. And the Pilgrims' firm stand impressed the Indians for miles around. Corbitant asked the Pilgrims' forgiveness. The Indians on Martha's Vineyard sent a group to make a peace treaty. Only the powerful Narragansett Indians remained hostile. The Narragansetts sent the Pilgrims a bundle of arrows wrapped in a snakeskin. Returning threat for threat, the Pilgrims' governor sent them a snakeskin filled with bullets and gunpowder.

It was high time, the Pilgrims decided, to fence in their village and lock it at night. This they did, with men taking turns standing guard.

The harvest that year was poor. Two shiploads of newcomers had arrived in June. With sixty more mouths to feed, the winter ahead looked bleak indeed.

When a ship stopped at Plymouth, with beads and knives to sell, the Pilgrims bought all they could. Then a group of men set out in the shallop to trade these for food from the Nauset Indians on Cape Cod.

Squanto died on this voyage of the "Indian Sickness." Before he died, he asked that his few belongings be divided among his friends at Plymouth.

By this time the Pilgrim children had become very fond of Squanto, and they missed

him. All of the Pilgrims mourned for the Indian who had helped them so much. But they accepted this loss, like all their misfortunes, as "God's will."

That autumn, the men who had come to Plymouth in June moved to the site of Weymouth, near Boston. There they started their own colony. For the most part these men were a lazy, dishonest lot, and soon they were stealing from the Indians.

This could only lead to trouble, so the Indians felt they must take action. Through their friend Massasoit, they learned that the Massachusetts tribe had joined forces with the Nausets of Cape Cod. Together they planned to wipe out the settlement at Weymouth. That done, they were going to attack Plymouth.

Soon afterward a Massachusetts Indian was found spying on Plymouth. Again Governor Bradford took swift action. Miles Standish and his men went to Weymouth. Several Indians were killed and the others routed. Captain Standish returned with an Indian head, which was mouted on the fort, in the custom of the day, to frighten enemies.

News of the foray spread all over. Some Indians who had planned to join the Massachusetts went into hiding. The Nauset chief died. Other tribes sent canoes loaded with gifts for Governor Bradford. There was no more

trouble with the Indians for many years.

In their dealings with the Indians, the Pilgrims tried to be fair and honest. But, like other settlers, they were taking land to which they had no true right. Except for Squanto, the Pawtuxet Indians were all dead, so no payment was made for Plymouth. Other Massachusetts land was paid for but usually with clothing or tools of little value.

To many Indians, selling land was something new and puzzling anyway. They thought it meant that the settlers could move in, not that they themselves must move out. When they found they were unwelcome, they often built new lodges nearby. They continued to hunt and fish on the land of their ancestors.

The Pilgrims' former minister in Holland heard of Miles Standish's clash with the Indians at Weymouth. It was too bad, he wrote, that they had not made the Indians into Christians before killing them.

The Pilgrims had done their best to impose their religion on all the Indians they knew. They wanted to "help" them. But the Indians had their own religion and tribal customs. As is now known, people are better off with their own beliefs and sacred customs. Robbed of these, they lose self-respect and become confused.

On Thanksgiving Day in 1972, a flag was

flown over the Capitol building in Washington, D.C., to honor the Wampanoag Indians. This was the tribe headed by Massasoit.

A year later, Asa Lombard IV, an eighty-one-year-old *Mayflower* descendant, presented the flag to eighty-one-year-old Wampanoag Chief Lorenzo Jeffers, in a ceremony at Mashpee, Massachusetts.

Chief Jeffers said that his ancestor, Massasoit, "as he gazed at the sky believed there was something superior to man. He realized that if he didn't treat the Pilgrims right, whoever was superior to man would not treat his people right."

The Chief also said that people must understand why the Indians and the white people acted as they did, because "this is the only way to create harmony."

At Thanksgiving time, on classroom walls, windows, blackboards, and bulletin boards, there are usually drawings and paintings of Indians and Pilgrims. November calendars sometimes picture them gathered for the feast that first autumn. Thanksgiving greeting cards, paper tablecloths, and napkins are often decorated with pictures of Indians and Pilgrims.

Shown together like this, they remind us that "the land of the Pilgrims' pride" was once really American Indian land.

The Thanksgiving Dinner Table

A family gathered around a festive dinner table is another favorite subject for Thanksgiving greeting cards. What other scene could express the spirit of the occasion better? For, more than any American holiday, Thanksgiving is a day of feasting.

Preparations for the feast start days ahead. Besides turkey, the shopping list might include sweet potatoes, onions, green peas or beans, squash, turnips, celery, cranberry sauce, nuts, fruits, and candies. Usually, there are also pies to be baked or bought.

The menu varies from family to family, but usually includes turkey, roasted golden brown and stuffed in all sorts of delicious ways.

At the Pilgrims' first feast, they ate their fill of wild turkey roasted over open fires. They

70

had plenty of venison, or deer meat, too, the nearest thing to the roast beef that they missed so much.

Perhaps they also ate fish, clams, oysters, and lobsters. But lobster and other shellfish were not the luxury to the Pilgrims that they are to us. Often, during their first year, they ate lobster and shellfish as much as three times a day.

Other kinds of fish would probably have been more to their liking. But the Pilgrims' hooks were too large to catch flounder and cod, and they had no nets.

Aboard the *Mayflower*, the Pilgrims had lived mainly on pickled salt beef or pork and hardtack. Few of them had fresh fruit or any vegetables to eat. The lack of vitamins caused the scurvy from which a number of them died that first winter.

Those still alive in the spring had been barely strong enough to plant the crops that were their only hope of surviving another year. Now, here before them was all this corn, all these pumpkins, and beans. What better way to celebrate than with a feast?

Planks set on sawhorses served as tables. Stools and tree stumps served as seats, at least for some. The Indians, and probably the children, sat on the ground.

Since human beings first harvested crops, there have been harvest feasts.

The ancient Greeks held a harvest festival in honor of Demeter, goddess of plant life and of farming. She was the mother of Persephone, goddess of seasons.

The ancient Romans called their harvest goddess, Ceres. Each autumn they honored her with the *Ceralia* festival.

At these autumn festivals, the Greeks and Romans feasted on nuts, fruits, and other harvest bounty. They reveled in the feeling of plenty.

Three thousand years ago, the Hebrew people settled in warm, sunny Palestine and became farmers. They plowed the soil and planted seed in February. By April the fields were green with ripe grain. Seven weeks after this first harvest, the Hebrews held the festival of *Shavuoth*. At that time some of the first figs and other fruits were taken to the temple.

Still celebrated today in the late spring, Shavuoth is also known as the Feast of Weeks. At some time in the history of the Jewish people, it came to stand for the day Moses received the Ten Commandments.

In Israel, Shavuoth is a joyful holiday. Young people march in parades. Ancient harvests are recalled by special songs and dances. The dancers go through the motions of reaping grain.

Another Jewish harvest festival handed down from ancient times is *Sukkoth*, the Feast of the Tabernacles. An autumn holiday, it goes on for eight days as it did in biblical times.

During the grape harvest the Hebrews slept at the vineyards to protect their grapes. Their shelters were crude booths made of branches. Today each autumn at the time of Sukkoth, people of the Jewish faith build similar shelters, called *succahs* or tabernacles.

The ancient Egyptians held a harvest festival in honor of Min, the god they believed made the earth fertile. In Egypt, as in Palestine, there was more than one harvest. The festival in honor of Min was held in the spring. The first sheaf of grain was cut by the Pharaoh or King. Since he was supposed to be a god himself, this act was meant to ensure plenty.

Ancient China held a harvest festival called *Hhung-Ch'iu*, the birthday of the moon. It came on the fifteenth day of the eighth month, when the Queen of the Night, as the moon was called, was at her brightest.

This was probably what the farmers of the western world called the harvest moon.

73

Lingering in the sky for several nights in a row, it flooded the earth below with bright moonlight. These moonlit nights were as good as an extra day or two for harvesting crops.

At the ancient Chinese festival, thanks were given for the harvest. On little altars in all the courtyards people placed round moon cakes and round fruits. At midnight, after a ceremony, each family celebrated with a moonlight feast.

During the rice harvest in Japan, some farmers still honor the field god of their ancestors. After the new rice is offered to their god, the people sample it themselves. With feasting and joyful celebration, they send the field god to the mountains to stay there until the following spring.

In Africa, many tribes still observe the harvest festivals of their ancestors. As the owners and guardians of the land, the ancestors are thanked for keeping the people well and for sending rain. To the ancestors go the first fruits of the harvest.

In India, most of the farming people have joyful harvest festivals, sometimes a different one for each crop. The first fruits of the land are offered to the gods. The dead are remembered, too. The people feast and enjoy a feeling of closeness to their ancestors, their gods, and the land.

74

Each September, Indian women of the Hindu religion hold a festival in honor of Gauri, goddess of the harvest and protector of women. A bundle of balsam carried by a young girl stands for the goddess. After a ceremony, Gauri is offered milk and sweets. On the second day the women enjoy a feast.

The Celtic people, who lived before the time of Christ in what is now France and the British Isles, held a festival each year around November 1. They called it *Samhain,* meaning summer's end. This was partly a harvest festival and partly a day of the dead. On Samhain Eve the ghosts of dead souls were supposed to come back, seeking warmth and shelter.

By this time, the grain had been reaped and stored. The cattle were in from the pasture. There was never enough fodder to feed all of them during the winter, so some animals were killed and eaten.

Rejoicing in the harvest, the Celtic people feasted, gave thanks, and remembered their ancestors with offerings of food.

Harvest festivals continued in Europe for centuries. Each country had customs of its own. In England the festival was called *Harvest Home*. In Scotland it was known as the *Kern*. The date varied from country to country, just as the time of the harvest varied.

On English farms, the reaper who cut the

last sheaf of grain might be named Lord of
the Harvest. With his sweetheart or wife, he
would ride home on top of the last load. Holding garlands of leaves or flowers, the other
farmhands would walk along beside the
wagon. There was lots of laughter, joking, and
songs such as this one:

> We have plowed, and we have sowed,
> We have reaped, and we have mowed,
> We have brought home every load,
> Hip, hip, hip, Harvest Home!

Everyone looked forward to a Harvest
Home supper of roast beef, suet pudding, and
other delicious dishes. Usually held in the
barn, the harvest supper was given by the
master and mistress of the farm.

76

As thanks for the largesse, the workers sang songs like this:

Here's health to our master,
    The Lord of the feast;
God bless his endeavors,
    And send him increase!

In time, reaping and harvesting machines took the place of sickle and scythe. And, with farm machines, came an end to the old harvest customs on most European farms. Instead, there was often a harvest festival for the whole parish. A church service would be followed by a dinner and an afternoon of sports.

Long before people from Europe set foot on American soil, the North American Indians had celebrated the harvest.

In South America the Incas and probably other Indians had held harvest festivals, too. South of the Equator the seasons are opposite from ours. In our May, which is autumn there, the Incas held a festival called *The Song of the Harvest.* They offered the first corn to their gods.

When our modern Thanksgiving became fixed as a November holiday, this was so close to harvest time that a feast always seemed in order. Gradually, the dinner became an important part of the day. People would go to church, then home to a feast.

In Massachusetts, on Thanksgiving morning, the pastors used to read the governor's Thanksgiving proclamation. Elbridge Gerry, who was governor from 1810 to 1812, wrote one that took more than two hours to read. When one pastor looked up after reading it, he found most of the pews empty. The church members, hungry for their dinners, had slipped out, one by one.

With its roots in former harvest festivals, when people gloried in a feeling of plenty, our American Thanksgiving has always been a day for sharing. Every year churches, clubs, classes, and other groups see to it that the needy and unfortunate have good dinners on Thanksgiving Day.

Indian Corn

All-cheering Plenty, with her
    flowing horn,
Led yellow Autumn, wreath'd with
    nodding corn.

Robert Burns

Cornstalks, ears of Indian corn, squash, pumpkins, and the nuts and fruits that ripen in autumn—all these form bright decorations for Thanksgiving Dinner napkins and for greeting cards of the holiday more devoted to feasting than any other.

Corn and pumpkins are symbols, too, of Halloween, which also has roots in ancient harvest festivals.

The Indian corn that the Pilgrims found on Cape Cod was buried in the sand. They dug some up, then came back for more, paying for it later on. Some of the corn they saved for planting the following spring.

At Plymouth, the first exploring party found "divers cornfields and running brooks."

Without the hoard of Indian corn and these cleared fields, the Pilgrims might not have survived. This was probably the only place on the whole eastern coast with some cleared ground and no Indians to object to the settlers using it.

79

Corn was new to the Pilgrims. In England and Holland, they had grown wheat, peas, and barley. Some of these they planted that first spring, but the English seed did poorly in alien soil.

The time to plant corn, Squanto said, was when the oak leaves were the size of a mouse's ear. He showed the Pilgrims how to hoe the earth into six-foot squares, then heap it into little hills.

Three or four kernels of corn were planted in every hill, with two or three fish for plant food. The fish were alewives, a kind of herring. In early spring, they swam upstream in large schools and were easy to catch.

Even with Squanto's help, the Pilgrims had trouble growing their corn. As we have read, the mastiff and spaniel dogs caught wind of the rotting fish and dug up the corn hills. The Pilgrims were forced to keep the dogs tied up until the corn was high. At night they took turns guarding the precious corn hills from prowling wolves.

To keep the Indians from knowing how many of the Pilgrims had died, corn was planted over the first graves.

When the corn ears were fully formed,

the stalks were cut and made into sheaves. Squanto said this was the best way to ripen corn.

Whether they liked corn or not, the Pilgrims were delighted with their bumper crop. It was like a proof or promise that they would survive.

The ears of Indian corn were rather small and knobby, with red, yellow, blue, green, and black kernels. Some of it the Pilgrims roasted and ate green. Most of it they dried for pounding into meal. This they made into corn bread or corn meal mush.

Just as the Pilgrims laughed at their rags and patches, they laughed at their troubles in growing corn. One stanza of a Pilgrim ballad goes:

When the spring opens and then we take
        the hoe,
And make the ground ready to plant
        and to sow;
Our corn being planted and seed being sown,
The worms destroy much before it is grown;
And when it is growing, some spoil
        there is made,
By birds and by squirrels that pluck
        up the blade;
E'en when it is grown to full corn in the ear,
It often is destroyed by raccoons and deer.

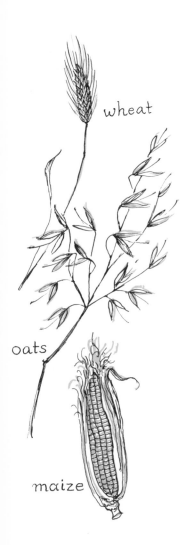

wheat

oats

maize

Corn or maize was first grown at least two thousand years ago, probably in Central America. Among the Mayan and Aztec Indians of Central America and the Incas of South America, corn was the main food. As such, it played a central role in their religion. They had special ceremonies for planting, for various stages of the corn's growth, and for the harvest.

The Iroquois Indians of North America still hold an annual Drum Dance of Thanksgiving. Among those who are thanked are the three sister spirits of the corn. The ceremony takes place in August, the Green Corn Month of the Iroquois.

The name *corn* really means the seeds of a cereal grass, especially the important cereal crop of a region. In England at the time of the Pilgrims this was wheat and, in Scotland and Ireland, oats. In the New World it was *maize* or Indian corn.

For centuries, many people of Europe believed in a Corn Mother. A kind of harvest goddess, she descended from the Greek Demeter and the Roman Ceres. The Corn Mother's spirit was said to dwell in the last sheaf of grain standing in a field.

To avoid killing the Corn Mother, the sheaf was beaten with sticks until all the seeds

82

were threshed out. This was said to prove that the Corn Mother had been driven out.

Sometimes the last sheaf of grain was made into the figure of a woman. Dressed and hung with flowers and ribbons, it rode to the granary with the last wagonload of grain. There it was placed in the threshing room to ensure a good harvest the following year.

In some places a Corn Maiden or Corn Child replaced the Corn Mother. Beliefs and customs, of course, varied greatly from place to place in Europe.

Though not usually found on the Thanksgiving menu, corn does have a place in the holiday. As at Halloween, cornstalks and ears of corn are often used as decorations at dinners and parties. And, at this time of year, bunches of multicolored Indian corn are a favorite decoration for house and apartment doors.

Pumpkins

In Thanksgiving decorations, pumpkins often appear with cornstalks and harvest vegetables. New England settlers used to say that corn, beans, and pumpkins or squash were the Indian Three Sisters, for these three were the Indians' main crops.

With the Indian corn that the Pilgrims dug up at Cape Cod, were some bags of dried beans. These, too, furnished seed that first spring in the New World.

Whether the Pilgrims ate pumpkin in any form at their first Thanksgiving is uncertain. But two years later, in 1623, they were eating more of it than they wanted—at least according to this stanza from one of their ballads:

Instead of pottage and puddings and
custard and pies,
Our pumpkins and parsnips are
common supplies;
We have pumpkin at morning and
pumpkin at noon,
If it were not for pumpkin, we should
be soon undoon.

Squanto had taught the Pilgrims to plant pumpkin seed in the spaces between the corn hills. The spreading pumpkin vines kept the weeds down and saved the people work.

Today pumpkin pie is a favorite Thanksgiving dessert. The only pies the Pilgrims knew were meat pies.

What the Pilgrims missed more than sweet things was the beer they were used to drinking with their meals. English beer had been made from barley. Once the Pilgrims had pumpkins, they made beer out of "pumpkins and parsnips, and walnut tree chips."

After apple trees were brought from England, cider replaced this beer as the Pilgrims' favorite beverage.

Tom Turkey

Of all the Thanksgiving symbols, the turkey is the only one that, by itself, suggests the holiday. This large, stately bird with its greenish bronze feathers and handsome fan is seen on Thanksgiving greeting cards, place cards, tablecloths, and napkins.

This is the Tom Turkey. As with other birds, the male has the brighter plumage. The hen turkey has drab feathers and is smaller.

Many stories of the Pilgrims' first harvest state flatly that roast turkey was part of the feast. Some of these stories go on to say that the birds were a gift from the Indian guests.

Governor Bradford, in his book about Plymouth, said that large numbers of water fowl and turkeys appeared at the approach of winter. He never said that they were eaten at the feast. He never described it.

The only account by someone who was there is in a letter that Pilgrim Edward Winslow sent to England. In it, he wrote that the governor had sent four men out fowling. In one day, he said, they brought back enough to feed everyone for about a week.

So, along with venison and fish, the Pilgrims and their Indian guests must have enjoyed roast turkey as well as duck and geese.

86

Wild turkeys feed on insects, seeds, berries, and tender plants, so the meat is more tasty than the flesh of water fowl that feed on fish.

During their second year at Plymouth, the Pilgrims had poultry brought from Europe and began raising hens and geese. Before long they had tamed the wild turkey and were raising these birds as well. The Pilgrims were not the first to do this. Tame Mexican turkeys had been brought to Europe by the Spaniards in 1519. By 1530 the bird was well known there.

Until this century, many American backyards held vegetable patches and hen coops. Families could raise their own chickens and their Thanksgiving turkey. Then, as towns grew larger and the standard of living rose, people began to buy their eggs and poultry.

For some time, though, chicken and turkey were a luxury that many families could afford only on important occasions. One of these was Thanksgiving.

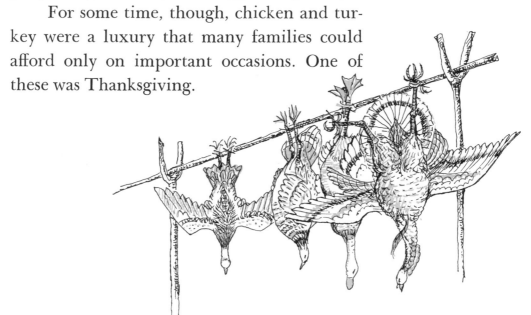

As time went on, prices of chicken and turkey dropped. Meanwhile the prices of beef, pork, lamb, and veal rose, making these meats more of a luxury.

Chicken meat is more popular than turkey, but for Thanksgiving turkey still reigns supreme.

Benjamin Franklin thought the turkey would have been a good symbol for our nation. He said:

> "I wish the Bald Eagle had not been chosen as the representative of our country; he is a Bird of bad moral character; like those among Men who live by Sharping and Robbing, he is generally poor and often very lousy. The Turkey is a much more respectable Bird and withal a true original Native of North America."

From Crane Berry to Cranberry

No American Thanksgiving dinner would seem complete without cranberries. In a sauce, jelly, or relish, the piquant flavor of cranberry adds exactly the right fillip to roast turkey.

Most cranberries grow on Cape Cod, and an old legend tells how this came to be. An Indian medicine man cast a spell over a certain minister and mired him in quicksand. Then he began boasting about the power of his medicine. The minister declared that his own brand of medicine, the Christian religion, was much stronger. To settle the argument they agreed to a fifteen-day battle of wits.

Bogged down in the quicksand all this time, the minister might have starved had it not been for a kind white dove. Every little while the white dove brought him a bright red berry.

The medicine man had no spell that worked on doves. Exhausted by thirst and hunger, the medicine man finally collapsed. His spell broke, and the minister was freed.

89

While this was going on, one of the red berries fell to the ground. There it took root and formed the start of the first cranberry bog.

A story like this shows how strongly the white settlers felt that there was really only one religion—their own.

Actually, the Indians introduced the Pilgrims to the sour red berries that grew in the bogs around Plymouth.

The Cape Cod Indians called the berry *Ibimi,* meaning bitter berry. To the Pilgrims, the nodding pink blossom of the plant looked like the head of a crane. So *crane berry* seemed like a good name for it. In time this name was changed to cranberry.

The Indians used cranberry poultices to draw the venom from arrow wounds. The bright red cranberry juice gave them a dye for rugs and blankets. Cranberries mixed with dried venison and fat formed a food the Indians called *pemmican.* Shaped into cakes and baked in the hot sun, it would keep for a long time.

The Pilgrims invented cranberry recipes of their own. They made cranberry sauce, cranberry tarts, cranberry nog, and a jam made of cranberries and apples, sweetened with syrup from pumpkin pulp.

After Plymouth and other settlements turned into thriving towns, cranberries remained popular. Each fall people gathered them to preserve for winter.

As trade with Europe grew, cranberries were served to ships' crews to provide them with the vitamin C that prevents scurvy.

Today, in the factories where cranberries are made into juice or jelly, the berries have to bounce over four-inch barriers. Each berry gets seven chances. In this way the soft ones are left behind.

In winter, the cranberry bogs around Plymouth are flooded to protect the vines. After ice forms, the water underneath is drained off. Under their blanket of ice, the cranberry vines can then "breathe."

Today, in Plymouth, children go ice skating on the frozen cranberry bogs.

And cranberries are still on the Thanksgiving menu—as they have been since the 17th century.

Horn of Plenty

Heap high the farmer's wintry hoard!
Heap high the golden corn!
No richer gift has Autumn poured
From out her lavish horn!

From the *Corn Song* by
John Greenleaf Whittier

No symbol so well expresses the harvest side of Thanksgiving as a horn overflowing with fruits, nuts, vegetables, and sometimes flowers. Since ancient times the horn of plenty has been a symbol of the earth's bounty.

The Greeks had several myths about *cornucopia,* their name for the horn of plenty. One of these tells of Amalthea, a goat who suckled the infant god Zeus. Once Amalthea broke off one of her horns. Filling it with fruits and flowers, she gave it to Zeus. To show his gratitude, Zeus later set the goat's image in the sky as the constellation Capricorn.

92

In another myth, Amalthea was a nymph who raised Zeus on goat's milk. The grateful young god broke off the goat's horn and gave it to his kind foster mother. This horn of plenty would supply her an abundance of whatever she wanted.

Gratitude for abundance is the keynote of the modern Thanksgiving as it was of the first harvest festivals.

At these early harvest festivals and at Thanksgiving dinners of the past, people feasted on food they had grown themselves. Today most of us dine on food grown far away and shipped to supermarkets. Even so, Thanksgiving still reminds us of how much we depend on the earth and helps to renew our ties with it.

And what ties could be more important? For, as the first book of the Bible says, "While the earth remaineth, seedtime and harvest, and cold and heat, and summer and winter, and day and night, shall not cease."

Thanksgiving Stories, Poems, Pageants, and Plays

Child, Lydia Maria. *Thanksgiving Day*. The old favorite that begins "over the river and through the wood." May be found in almost any anthology of holiday poems such as *Poetry for Holidays*. Selected by Nancy Larrick. Illustrated by Kelly Oechsli. Champaign, Illinois: Garrard Publishing Company, 1968. It also serves as the text of a picture book, *Over the Hill and Through the Wood*. Illustrated by Brinton Turkle. New York: Coward, 1974.

Fisher, Aileen. *Skip Around the Year*. Illustrated by Gioia Fiammenghi. New York: Thomas Y. Crowell Company, 1967. Contains three charming, original Thanksgiving poems suitable for younger children.

Hall, Elvajean. *Margaret Pumphrey's Pilgrim Stories*. Revised and expanded by Elvajean Hall. Illustrated by Jon Nielsen. Chicago: Rand McNally & Company, 1961. Based on fact, interestingly written, and suitable for children of elementary school age.

Janice. *Little Bear's Thanksgiving*. Illustrated by Mariana. New York: Lothrop, Lee & Shepard Company, 1967. An amusing tale to read aloud to younger children or for beginning readers to enjoy by themselves.

Luckhardt, Mildred Correll, Compiler. *Thanksgiving Feast and Festival*. Illustrated by Ralph McDonald. Nashville. Abingdon Press, 1966. A rich collection of stories, poems, essays, and factual accounts. Includes well-known favorites as well as new selections, with good representation of various religious and ethnic groups. For readers of about 9 and up.

Sechrist, Elizabeth Hough and Woolsey, Janette. *It's Time for Thanksgiving*. Illustrated by Guy Fry. Philadelphia: Macrae Smith Company, 1957. Containing both religious and secular material, the book includes the history of the holiday, stories, poems, plays, games, and recipes for Thanksgiving treats. For children of about 6 to 10.

Weisgard, Leonard. *The Plymouth Thanksgiving*. Illustrated by the author. Garden City, N.Y.: Doubleday & Company, 1967. A beautiful picture book with a simple and vivid text. For readers of about 7 to 9, or for reading to younger children.

94

Sources

Bible. King James Version. Oxford, England: Oxford University Press, 1841.

Bradford, William. *Of Plymouth Plantation, 1620–1647*. Samuel Eliot Morison, ed. New York: Knopf, 1952.

Bulfinch, Thomas. *Bulfinch's Mythology*. New York: Thomas Y. Crowell Co.

Chambers, Robert, ed. *Book of Days*. Detroit: Gale Research Co., 1967 (Repr. of 1886 ed.).

Colby, Jean Poindexter. *Plimouth Plantation: Then and Now*. New York: Hastings House, 1952.

Frazer, James G. *The Golden Bough*. New York: St. Martin's Press, Inc., 1914.

Hall, Elvajean. *Pilgrim Stories*. (A revision of the Margaret Pumphrey Stories.) Chicago: Rand McNally, 1964.

Hazeltine, Mary E. *Anniversaries and Holidays*. 2nd ed. Chicago: American Library Association, 1944.

Luckhardt, Mildred Corell, ed. *Thanksgiving—Feast and Festival*. New York: Abingdon, 1966.

Morison, Samuel Eliot. *The Story of the "Old Colony" of New Plymouth, 1620–1692*. New York: Knopf, 1956.

Mourt's *Relation*. Heath, Dwight B., ed. *A Journal of the Pilgrims at Plymouth*. New York: Corinth Books, American Experience Series # 19.

Smith, E. Brooks and Meredith, Robert. *The Coming of the Pilgrims*. Boston: Little, Brown and Co., 1964.
— *Pilgrim Courage*. Boston: Little, Brown and Co., 1962.

Starkey, Marion L. *Land Where Our Fathers Died: The Settling of the Eastern Shores, 1607–1735*. Garden City, N.Y.: Doubleday & Co., Inc., 1962.

Willison, George F. *Saints and Strangers*. New York: Reynal & Hitchcock, 1945.

Wright, Arthur R. *British Calendar Customs*. Craus Reprints, 1968.

Index

(7 DAY- THANKSGIVING)

J
• 394.268
B

Barth
    Turkeys, Pilgrims,
and Indian corn

Date Due

NOV 10 '77	NOV 12 '87		
NOV 20 '78	DEC 09		
DEC 1 '80	NOV 15 '90		
DEC 9 '80	NOV 20 '91		
DEC 7	NOV 25 '97		
AUG 31 '82	DEC 23 '94		
NOV 23 '82	NOV 0 9 1998		
DEC 5 '83	NOV 28 2009		
DEC 6 '84			
DEC 2 '85			
DEC 16			